82

SMALL NEEDLEPOINT TREASURES

BY THE SAME AUTHORS

The Needlepoint Alphabet Book
Kids' Clothes by Meredith Gladstone
Small Needlepoint Treasures

SMALL NEEDLEPOINT TREASURES

A Complete How-to Workbook for Making Quick Needlepoint Gifts

BY MEREDITH GLADSTONE
Photographs by Gary Gladstone

WILLIAM MORROW & COMPANY, INC.

First Morrow Quill Paperback Edition
Copyright © 1979 by Meredith Gladstone and Gary Gladstone

DESIGNED BY ANTLER & BALDWIN, INC.

Library of Congress Cataloging in Publication Data
Gladstone, Meredith.   Small needlepoint treasures.
Includes index.   1. Canvas embroidery. I. Title.
TT778.C3G56   746.4′4   78-23750
ISBN 0-688-03388-1   ISBN 0-688-08388-9 pbk.

Printed in the United States of America.

First Edition

1 2 3 4 5 6 7 8 9 10

Contents

Introduction

My love for needlepoint never ends. I'm always on the lookout for some new thing to expand my needlepoint world—new materials, new uses of traditional materials, new designs, new uses for the needlepoint itself—testing ideas I haven't tried before. Every time I think I've explored all the avenues, something else appears and opens all sorts of new doors. The more I discover, the more I realize there *is* to discover, that the possibilities will never be exhausted.

I might exhaust myself, however! So I began thinking in terms of small projects to experiment with and see quickly if the ideas will work. Small objects also make marvelous gifts for others that they will truly treasure, and getting your project out of the house can be a good idea if your own house and family have been needlepointed to the brim as mine have. I decided to use a smaller mesh size of canvas, too, so I could get more detail into little areas. I tried new types of yarn and stitched in small fake pearls that had always intrigued me. My interest in print fabrics continues, as they are not only great design sources for pattern, but they are also terrific to combine with a finished piece of needlepoint. A fabric-covered wooden box with a needlepoint top makes a perfect gift and doesn't take long to make. Cover a notebook with fabric, and put a needlepoint pocket on it. Make a choker, bracelet, belt, or bookmark, using a fancy ribbon or fabric for backing, and trim it with beads. A needlepoint mat for a picture can become a wedding sampler or a birth announcement designed with names and dates stitched in. If I seem to jump around or get carried away, it's because the untried possibilities are as exciting as the "treasures" already planned or finished.

One of my favorite yarns has always been cotton embroidery floss. It's a smooth, silky 6-strand yarn with a beautiful luster. Because it's a natural fiber, it takes color beautifully, and the color range is magnificent. Several companies make this type of yarn, but the one that seems very good is a French one from the DMC Corporation. What Paternayan is to wool, DMC is to cotton. They make a color card that is usually on display where the yarn is sold. It looks like a huge Mexican serape, and I'm often tempted to frame the card itself. Along with a large range of solid colors, there are shaded yarns available that go from a light tone of a color to a dark one in the same thread and give a marvelous air-brush effect when stitched onto canvas. I like to use it for some backgrounds and for solid letters. This yarn is readily available in most department and specialty stores.

When I decided to try embroidery floss on needlepoint canvas, my first attempt was on 14-mesh-per-inch penelope canvas. I loved the effect of the cotton, but, since the yarn wasn't quite heavy enough to cover the canvas, I separated another piece and added strands to the first one to make it thicker. This works the same way as when you split 3-ply Persian wool and makes the same floss adaptable to several different mesh sizes of canvas. When it is worked up, the floss looks flat and silky, as opposed to wool, which has no shine and is "hairy."

I wanted to make something with my new discovery that wouldn't take much time, so I decided to try a decorative mat for a photo of my son Gregory to present to "Grampy" for Christmas. Once I decided on the design, the execution was relatively quick, and the results were terrific. Grampy was thrilled with his personalized photo of his grandson, and now Grandma, Nana, Aunt Patti, and Uncle Maurice each have their own special framed photos.

I used a standard Dax plastic box frame and placed the needlepoint mat inside, then the photo, then the cardboard backing that comes with the frame. The cardboard as it was looked dreary in contrast to the elaborate mat, so I decided to decorate the cardboard backing too. A cotton gingham with small checks picking up one of the yarn colors from the mat design was perfect. I covered the cardboard entirely with the fabric by simply gluing it on. I loved the effect, and it suggested all sorts of possibilities for other combinations.

Try incorporating fabrics into your designs. For instance, if you have a piece of printed fabric and particularly like its pattern, take the colors of one of the motifs, and use them on the needlepoint canvas as a mat for a photo. Use the fabric itself to cover the frame. You now have two different textures that work together to complement each other. The needlepoint has a raised effect from the stitches and is shiny from the yarn. The fabric is smooth and flat. The colors and pattern on both relate and tie them together. My next projects included a needlepoint mat set into a fabric-covered frame, then a needlepoint frame with a fabric-covered mat, and so on. Once a project is finished, it inspires me to take something in it that I like and reuse it in a slightly different way for something else.

Along with discovering new materials and projects, I'm constantly looking for new design sources. I do this automatically by now, and my clipping file bulges with new inspirations. I love alphabets. Gary and I discovered old woodcut letters that look amazingly modern. Old Victorian designs are perfect sources for picture mats. Swatches of fabrics, color cards, everything you love can find a use. In this book I hope to present you with new inspiration for designs and show you new techniques for using them. With 61 new life-size alphabets and patterns to trace, ideas for different materials to use and different needlepointed gifts to make, you should be able to try all sorts of new things. Use your own ideas and combine them with mine. Use the book as a springboard; jump in and have fun!

SMALL NEEDLEPOINT TREASURES

Materials, Tools, Stitches & Techniques

CANVAS

For all the projects in this book, I recommend needlepoint canvas ranging from 14 mesh to 18 mesh per inch. All of the designs can be traced directly from the book onto canvas within this range of mesh sizes. It's up to you to choose the one that works best for you. Both mono and penelope canvases will work. The important thing to remember for very small projects is to find canvas of the finest and lightest *weight,* so that it is pliable to work with and fine enough for the yarn to cover the canvas threads. Penelope canvas is generally lighter in weight because it is woven with two fine threads instead of one heavy one, but there is also fine mono canvas, particularly in the higher mesh counts. If you use mono canvas, try to find one that has a locked weave so that the threads stay in place. When deciding what mesh size to use for which projects, remember that you can get more detail on higher-count canvas. For a book cover or a larger object, I'll use 14- or 15-mesh canvas. Higher-count (18-mesh) canvas renders more detail and works up more slowly than lower-count (14-mesh), which gives less detail and works up more quickly. One canvas that works quite well is a 17-mesh one that comes in a cream color, is 43″ wide, and may be ordered from Elsa Williams, West

Needlepoint canvas from 14 to 18 mesh, in both mono and penelope

* This firm has a catalog you can buy and will send you the name of the shop nearest you that carries Elsa Williams products.

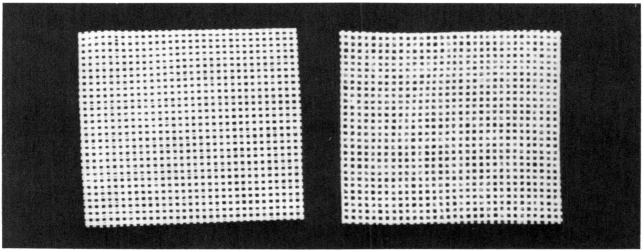

14-mesh

15-mesh

16-mesh

17-mesh

18-mesh

YARNS

Townsend, Massachusetts 01474.* I also like a fine 14-mesh penelope canvas that is white and 36″ wide. Not all sizes are always in stock, so I suggest you check out your local store to see what it has that you think might be best for you to work with. If you're not sure, experiment with different types and sizes to see which you prefer.

For all the projects, I have used predominantly an all-cotton, 6-strand embroidery floss packaged in small skeins in lengths of approximately 9 yards, or

Cotton embroidery floss

8 meters. As with wool yarns, there are different qualities. The finer, silkier cotton yarns are generally imported and stitch up better than the domestic ones, which are bulkier and coarser and have a tendency to snarl or knot while you work with them. The imports such as DMC have a wide color range and are available in most department and craft stores. The domestic ones are available in most dime stores, but do not have a very large color range. Dye lots in cotton floss do not vary as much as they do in wool, but since the skeins are small and inexpensive, always buy a few more than you need so you won't run short. I always have more than I need, and in order to keep them organized, I keep ranges of each color together with a rubber band and take out the skeins only as I need them. All of the blues are together, all the reds, and so on. The floss can be used as is (6 strands), for higher-count canvas (17- or 18-mesh) or can be made thicker and heavier by adding more strands. I usually use 8 strands for 16-mesh canvas and 9 strands for 14- and 15-mesh. These figures are suggested as a rough guide, because the number of strands you need also depends on the type of canvas you have. Generally, mono canvas requires heavier yarn than penelope. To make sure the floss covers the canvas, always test it by making a few sample stitches. If you need to make the floss thicker, cut 2 lengths of it each about 30″ long, and split one of them so you have 3 strands. Add the 3 strands to the 6 strands and thread the needle, making sure all the strands lie smoothly together. Save the other 3

13

strands and combine them with another 6-strand length. To make 8 strands use the same method, but split the second strand so that you have 3 lengths of 2 strands each. When splitting cotton floss, it's easier to separate the strands from the center and work out to each end so the strands won't tangle. It takes about 3 yards of floss to cover 1 square inch of canvas. When buying floss, I

Different mesh sizes of canvas stitched with different thicknesses of cotton floss

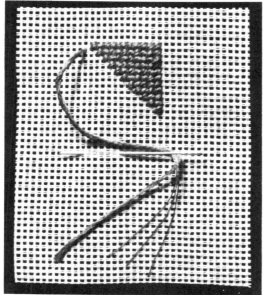

14-mesh 9 strands

16-mesh 8 strands

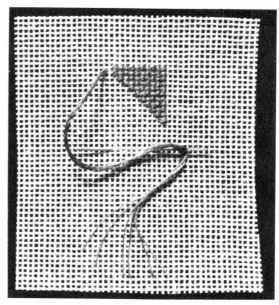

17-mesh as is (6 strands)

estimate that one skein covers 1½ to 2 square inches of canvas. Use this as a general guide to estimate what you need for a project.

Guide for Number of Strands and Coverage on Canvas

CANVAS SIZE	NO. OF STRANDS
14 and 15 mesh	9 strands (6 plus 3)
16 mesh	8 strands (6 plus 2)
17 and 18 mesh	6 strands (as is)

1 skein (9 yards or 8 meters) = 1½ square inches of stitched canvas

There are other types of embroidery yarn available. Other variations of cotton—slightly heavier and twisted ones—are good for backgrounds but are limited in color. There is also a rayon yarn that is very shiny and is great for small touches, though it has a tendency to ravel and tangle while being worked. There are silver, gold, and other metallic yarns that are also good for small touches. Any embroidery yarn that looks interesting to you should be tried; because they are generally sold in small quantities, it's no problem to buy a little to experiment with.

You can, of course, also use the old standby, wool, for any of the projects. Use 3-strand Persian so you can separate the strands: 2 strands for 14-

and 15-mesh canvas, 1 strand for 16-, 17-, and 18-mesh. In a few cases, especially the mini-pillows, I have used wool for the background, in combination with cotton floss for the design.

NEEDLES

For all the projects I use a #22 or #24 tapestry needle with the floss and #20 with wool. I usually prefer the smaller size #24 for all mesh sizes of canvas, but test to see what works best for you.

THIMBLE & SCISSORS

I recommend a thimble to save fingers and a small pair of very sharp, pointed scissors. Since you'll be working with fine canvas and floss that doesn't stretch the way wool does, sharp, pointy scissors in good condition are essential. I have snipped canvas threads several times when ripping out because either I was impatient or the scissors weren't sharp enough. When you are ripping out or correcting mistakes, take special pains so that you don't snip the canvas threads.

NEEDLEPOINT STITCHES

When working with cotton floss, I recommend sticking to the basic needlepoint stitch, using either the continental or basketweave version. Details of the smaller designs can be achieved best with this small stitch. Cotton floss does not lend itself to long stitches, because it doesn't have the fullness that wool has and won't cover the canvas. If you want to use some novelty stitches, I suggest you make a sample to see if they work in floss. Wool can always be used in place of, or in combination with, the floss.

You can add stitch interest to your designs by using embroidery stitches on top of the finished needlepoint. This adds texture and detail. For line stitches, use 2 strands of floss and a crewel embroidery needle, about #5. For French knots or anything you want to appear heavier, use 4 to 6

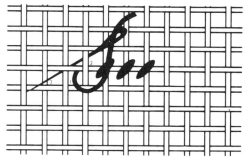

Continental stitch

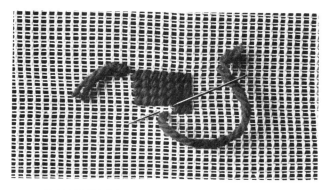

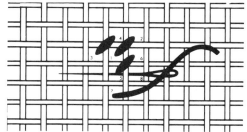

Basketweave (stitching up the canvas)

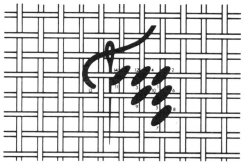

Basketweave (stitching down the canvas)

strands. Use the embroidery stitches suggested next to decorate your work. Outline areas that you want to separate; add shade lines to letters; use French knots for centers; experiment. . . .

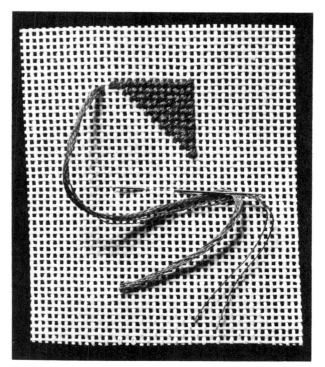

Basketweave stitch

EMBROIDERY STITCHES

1. The OUTLINE or STEM stitch. I use this to outline areas or draw fine lines. It can be used to separate colors as in a fan of colors, or to outline something as in the Christmas angel on page 47. Two strands of floss work best.

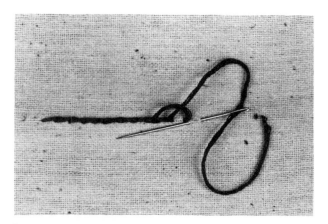

Outline or stem stitch

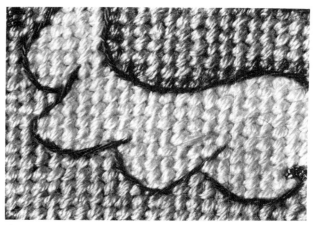

Outline or stem stitch

2. The BACKSTITCH. This stitch does basically what the outline stitch does, but it is smaller. Use 3 strands of floss.

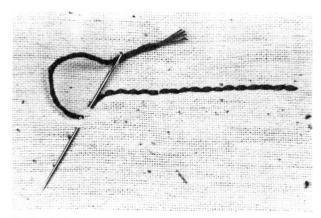

Backstitch

Backstitch

3. FRENCH KNOT. These are great for decorative spots and can be used individually or in clusters.

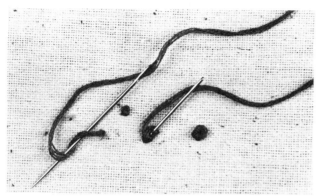

French knot

Outline or stem stitch and French knots

BEADS

Small beads can be used to add detail and texture. They can be found in most craft stores and are made in a wide variety of colors and sizes. They can be used in place of a stitch or can be stitched on top of the finished work.

If you want to use them in place of a stitch, stitch the beads in before the background. Pick beads that are approximately the size of one stitch; one bead should cover two crossed threads of the canvas the same way one yarn stitch does. You will need a beading needle, which is long and skinny so the beads will slip over it. Use 1 or 2 strands of floss, and work them on using the continental or half-cross stitch, slipping a bead on the floss in the middle of the stitch. Here is what you do: After securing the yarn to the back of your work, put the threaded needle through the canvas and out the front. Take a bead and slip it onto the needle, put the needle into the canvas where the rest of the stitch would go, and pull the yarn through tightly enough to secure the bead. Continue working as many beads as you want this way, then stitch in the background. If you want to add the beads on top of finished stitching, simply sew them on wherever you want them, making sure the threads don't show. Experiment with beads in a design the same way you would with yarns and colors.

NOTE: Do not put beads behind glass as the work won't stay flat.

Beads that take the place of stitches

Beads sewn on top of finished stitching

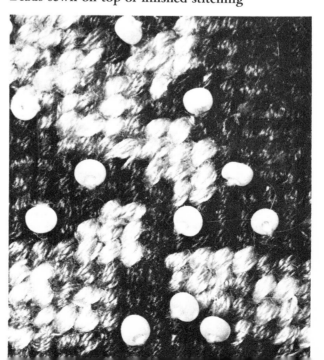

BUTTONHOLE-EDGE STITCH

For edges on projects where I want a neat, clean finish, I have borrowed the standard buttonhole stitch and used it for needlepoint. This is the stitch that you see around the edge of handmade buttonholes. For the cut-out on a mat or a frame, the edge of a belt, or anyplace where you want an edge to be flat and neat, it works very well; it can be used on any edge, regardless of the shape of a piece, and works as well on a curve as it does on a straight line. Your piece should always be blocked before you finish the edge, and you should use the same color yarn as you used along the edge of the needlepoint.

Once the piece is blocked, cut away the excess canvas, leaving ¼″ to ½″ around the edge. Turn back the canvas, pinching it between your fingers

The buttonhole stitch will finish both curved and straight edges.

Cutting away the excess canvas

Buttonhole stitch

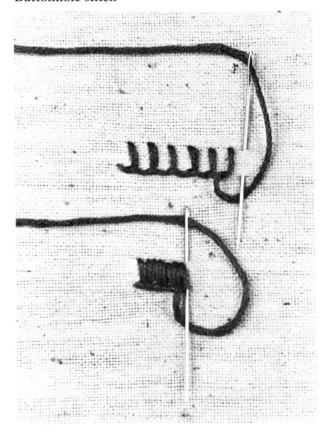

18

Securing the yarn at the back

Working the buttonhole-stitch edge, from the front

to keep it flat. Using the floss as is (6 strands), run it through the back of the needlepoint stitches to secure it and come up at the edge. Take small buttonhole stitches and keep them close together.

Use a fairly long strand of floss so that the stitch will be continuous for as long a distance as possible. When you have completed the edge, or come to the end of the yarn, run stitches through the back to secure the yarn.

NOTE: You can use either a tapestry or a crewel needle for this stitch. The crewel needle has a sharp point and will push through most easily if the edge of the work is thick. The buttonhole stitch does not work well in wool yarn, because wool stretches and breaks when it is constantly pulled back and forth to make the stitch.

FABRICS

When, to add interest to your design, you use fabric in conjunction with needlepoint, remember that flat cotton fabrics are the ones that work best for covering boxes, books, frames, or mats. (Wallpaper or decorative wrapping paper can also be used.) Finished needlepoint can also be applied to surfaces, but, since needlepoint is not as flexible as fabric, I suggest using it only on flat areas. Flat surfaces, as opposed to curves or surfaces with grooves, are the easiest to cover. Wooden surfaces for boxes and frames are also best, as glue does not adhere as well to plastic, and pins cannot be used to help control the finishing.

For covering surfaces, you'll need a small flat brush, pushpins, Elmer's glue, a container such as a small bowl to hold the glue and brush, a sharp mat knife or single-edge razor, and newspaper on your work area so glue doesn't get all over everything. Add a few drops of water to the glue in the bowl until the glue has an easily spreadable consistency.

COVERING A FRAME

Remove the backing and glass from the frame. Cut a piece of fabric about 2″ larger all around than the frame itself, and cut a small "X" in the center for orientation.

Pour glue into the container, add water as needed, and spread the glue with the brush on the

The glue-covered frame face down on the fabric, ready to be covered

front and sides of the frame. Place the frame, gluey front side down, on the wrong side of the fabric, centering it evenly all around.

Cut out the center, starting at the "X" and leaving about 1″ of fabric around the inside edge of the frame. Cut 45° angled slits into the inside corners, so the fabric can be turned back and stay flat. Cut out right angles at the outside corners. Using your fingers to smooth the fabric, press it onto the frame, first along one inside edge; trim the excess fabric with a razor. Do the same on the outside edge, and continue for the remaining 3 sides of the frame. If the glue dries while you're working, put more on when needed. When bringing the fabric around to the back, cut angles at the corners so the fabric meets or slightly overlaps. Make sure all the edges are glued down securely. If necessary, touch up the edges with more glue. Let it dry thoroughly. The glue will not discolor the fabric when it has dried.

The frame, seen from the back, one side covered and trimmed, the next ready to be covered

TO COVER THE BACKING OF A STANDING FRAME

Pull out the backing from the frame, cut a piece of fabric ½″ larger than the backing all around, and snip off the corners at an angle. Cut two slits at right angles to each other in the fabric for the stand piece to go through. Spread glue on the frame backing, slip the fabric over the stand piece, and press the fabric smoothly in place. Turn the edges of the fabric over onto the front of the frame backing and glue them down.

To cover the stand piece, make a paper pattern by slipping a piece of paper under it and tracing around the edges. Fold the paper along the longest edge, and cut out a double pattern, allowing ½″ extra all around the cut sides. Using the pattern, cut out the fabric. Spread glue on both sides of the stand piece, and place the fabric on the top side first. Turn under the edges, and then bring the fabric around to cover the underside. Trim the under edges and touch up with glue.

Fabric laid on frame backing, slit twice to accommodate the stand piece

COVERING A FRAME WITH NEEDLEPOINT

Although the technique is basically the same for covering a frame with fabric or needlepoint, there are special details to be considered when you are working with needlepoint. The frame should be rather wide, flat, and made of wood. At the very beginning you must make a paper pattern of the area to be covered, and it must be accurate so that frame and needlepoint will fit together.

To make the pattern, place a piece of paper over the frame as if to cover it. Cut out the center and cut slits in each corner so the paper can be folded back. Use pushpins to hold it in place, and fold the paper back along all the edges, inside and outside. Remove the paper, mark the fold lines with pencil, and use this as a pattern for the needlepoint area. Check to make sure the lines are straight and the corners squared. Work out your

Finishing the covering of the stand piece

Starting the paper pattern for the needlepoint area that will cover a frame

Finished needlepoint frame. Enough extra rows of needlepoint have been stitched, inside and outside, to cover the turnover of all the edges.

design to size on another piece of paper, transfer it to canvas, then stitch and block the canvas. Add a few extra rows of needlepoint, outside and inside, for extra turnback. Once the needlepoint has been blocked, cut out the center, trim the edges, and apply it to the frame, using the same techniques you would for fabric. Use pushpins to keep the needlepoint straight as you work.

COVERING A MAT WITH FABRIC

To make a fabric mat, cut a piece of mat or poster board the same size as the glass. Then cut out the opening or openings you want. To cover the mat, cut out the fabric the same size as the mat or slightly larger; it can be trimmed after it's applied and no turnover is needed on the outside edges. Make an "X" cut in the center of the opening or openings. Cut the fabric out of the openings, leav-

ing ½" to ¾" around the edges to turn under. For a square opening, cut angled slits into the corners. For an oval or round opening, cut slits all around. Apply glue to the mat, place the fabric on it, and spread it flat. Turn the mat over, put glue around the edges of the openings, and turn the fabric edges back, pressing them in place with your fingers so they lie smooth and flat.

To make a needlepoint mat, you must make a paper pattern first so that you know the exact area to be covered.

Left, starting an oblong fabric mat; right, the turnback of an oval mat ready to be glued

COVERING A BOX WITH FABRIC

The same technique used to cover a frame is used for a box. The differences are that the sides are deeper and there is no center to cut out.

Cut a piece of fabric 1" larger than needed. For a box, this means that you'll need the surface measurement and the side measurements plus the 1" extra all around to turn over the lip of the box.

The top and bottom of the box are both covered the same way. Spread glue on the bottom (top) of the box, and place fabric on it, making sure it's centered. Cut out angles at the corners, allowing a little fabric for overlapping at the corners. Spread the sides of the box with glue, and press the fabric flat to all sides. Work two opposite sides completely, and then the other two, so that the corners are sure to be covered. To hold the sides in place, use pushpins (leave until the glue dries). Put glue on the lip and along the inside edges. Angle the corners, press the fabric over and down, and trim excess. Allow to dry. Use the same technique for the inside of a box or to cover the cardboard backing that goes inside a plastic box frame.

Fabric ready to cover box, with 1″ extra fabric at the outside edge of each flap

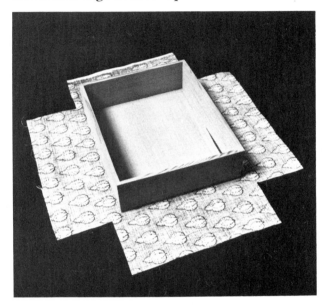

Box in progress, with angles cut in the fabric at the corners for a smooth fit

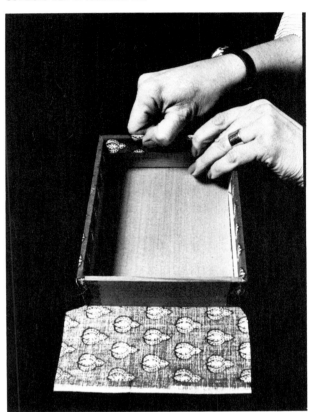

For a needlepoint cover, you must first make an accurate pattern of the area to be stitched in needlepoint.

Setting Up Your Design

All the designs in this book can be traced freehand from the printed page. That is to say, they require no graphing and can all be drawn by hand onto canvas and interpreted to fit your own requirements. For the beginner, there are design projects that can be copied exactly. For the more experienced or more daring, there are graphic ideas that can be lifted and changed to develop original designs.

For whatever project you choose, there are two essential steps: The first is to make a paper pattern of the area to be stitched in needlepoint. The second step is to make your design pattern, which gives you the design itself to be traced onto canvas.

MAKING A PAPER PATTERN

Once you decide what you want to make, you'll need a pattern of the area to be covered in needlepoint. To make this you need plain paper (a piece larger than the area to be covered), pencils, a ruler, and tracing paper. If you're making something that must fit your own dimensions, different from the ones given for projects in the book, you must make your own paper pattern. For any object that isn't absolutely flat, a pattern is necessary so your needlepoint will cover it properly. To illustrate, I'll explain how to make a paper pattern for an album cover. This will be more complicated than a flat picture mat, so it is a good example of how to make a pattern for anything that is three dimensional.

Start with a plain piece of paper that will go around the album with extra to spare. You may also use tracing paper to do this; see photo. Place the album open flat on the paper, and trim the paper so there is about 2″ extra all around. Fold the paper around the album, close the album, and make sharp creases along each vertical side of the binding. To get the creases flat, use a ruler and press it along the folds. Now fold in the paper edges and press flat. Then crease the paper along the binding at the

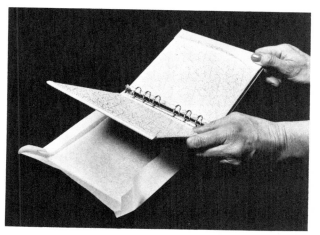

Folded paper pattern for covering an album; it may be made of any plain paper or of tracing paper.

top and bottom, and fold in and press flat. Take the paper off, and go over all the fold lines with pencil and a ruler so they are perfectly straight and square. Now place a piece of tracing paper over the paper pattern, and trace all the lines. The finished design will fit inside these lines, but add about ½″ extra for border stitching all around for turnback. You now have your paper pattern for the album cover. The same folding and tracing technique can be used for any other three-dimensional shape built on right angles that you may want to cover. For a simple flat area, just draw your dimensions on paper and you have your pattern.

MAKING A DESIGN PATTERN

Once you have your paper pattern traced onto tracing paper, you're ready to make your design pattern. Fill in the area with a rough sketch of the design. By working out ideas on tracing paper, you have a chance to correct, retrace, and try different elements together before committing anything to canvas. For your design pattern, make sure you have a pencil, eraser, and a black pen to make final lines heavy enough so they can be seen for tracing when the canvas is placed over the pattern. Do the rough sketching in pencil. You can also color in the sketch later if you wish, with crayons, colored pencils, felt pens, or paints.

In each section of this book there are suggested designs for specific projects. Use the cover photographs for color suggestions.

Trace the design directly, or use it as a source of inspiration. For instance, a design suggested for a picture mat could become a pillow; instead of a cutout for a photo in the center, put in an initial or a monogram, and back and stuff the piece as a pillow. Or a pillow design can be made into a piece for framing. Different designs can be worked together, with a motif from one combined with a motif from another. By using tracing paper, you can trace different pieces of designs together to get an idea how they will look before you make a master tracing. Try several design patterns to see which you like best. Once you've decided upon your design, make heavy black pen lines over your final outlines. If you don't get your pen lines quite right at this point, you can always retrace again onto fresh tracing paper or onto the original paper pattern if that was made with tracing paper.

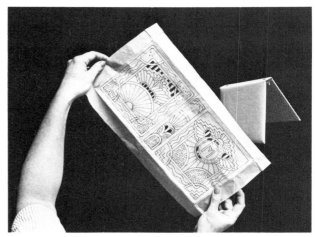

Album design pattern outlines traced onto tracing-paper paper pattern

Treat your outlined drawing as a page from a coloring book and paint in the colors. You can lay another piece of tracing paper over the drawing and paint in colors. Try as many color sketches as you need until you're happy with the results. By putting your colors on the paper, you don't need to put them on the canvas because you can use the sketch as your color guide. Use this to choose your yarn.

You will in some cases want to put in names and/or dates. They should be drawn in their spaces

Tracing letters from the printed alphabet

so that they are centered evenly. Let's take a picture mat for the example, with the name put in using the script alphabet. On a piece of tracing paper, draw a straight line, using a ruler. Place the paper over the alphabet and trace each letter needed to spell out the name, spacing carefully between the letters so the name looks neat and even. In this project of mine it is "The Goldmans." Once it is traced, find the center of the line of type, and draw a vertical line. This center line should match up with the center guideline on the space, here a ribbon, in which the name is to be fitted. Place the tracing of the photo mat over the name, matching the center lines. The ribbon is slightly curved, so move the name as you trace to follow the contour of the ribbon. Once the tracing is done, go over the letters with a black pen so they will all be visible for tracing onto canvas.

Tracing the name into its space on the design pattern of a picture mat

TRANSFERRING THE DESIGN TO CANVAS

Cut a piece of canvas for your design, allowing about 1″ extra on all sides. Bind the edges with masking tape to prevent raveling and/or catching on your yarns. Tape the design pattern in place on your work surface so it doesn't slip around, and

The design traced onto canvas from the design pattern

place the canvas over it, making sure it's centered and straight. Tape the canvas in place, too, so it doesn't slide around while you're tracing. Use a pointed waterproof pen to copy the design.

The best pen I have found is made by PILOT and is called "SC-UF ultra fine point permanent." It comes in black, red, green, and blue and can be found in most art-supply and stationery stores. It is relatively inexpensive (about 60¢ at the moment) and very colorfast. The fine point makes tracing small details easy. I always buy several at a time to be sure there is always one with a sharp point available, as the points will dull as you use them. I always use the black one to trace. You should also have a pen with a broader tip, also colorfast, to make heavy or shaded lines.

Trace the design on the canvas. If I can't see the design too clearly, I work over a light table. Taping design and canvas to a window with daylight behind it, or to a glass table top with a light under it, will give the same results.

You are now ready to stitch.

The
Projects

he projects appear in the book according to size, starting with the smallest and working up to the largest. Each type of project has variations using the same basic technique. For instance, a name tag can become a belt simply by being made longer. The main types are:

I.D. TAGS–luggage tags, key rings

STRIPS–Belts, napkin rings, chokers, bracelets, bookmarks, paperweights

COVERS, HOLDERS–Bookends, paper holders, coin purses, makeup holders, sachets

CHRISTMAS ORNAMENTS–pincushions, coasters, sachets

MATS, FRAMES

BOXES

ALBUM COVERS

MINI-PILLOWS

NOTE: There are finished items manufactured that have areas to fill in with needlepoint–totes, photo albums, and so on. One mail-order source that has very good things is Ellly, P.O. Box 304-CT, Guilford, Connecticut 06437. There is a small catalog that lists all the available items.

There are certain basic materials you'll need for all the projects, so I'll list them here. Other, special things you might need, as well as the basics, will be noted for each project.

A pad of tracing paper–9″ × 12″ or larger (to make patterns and lay out designs)

Pencils, erasers, rulers, compass (tools to sketch with)

Permanent black pens–PILOT pen SC-UF ultra fine point permanent black; also a broader-tipped pen (for tracing designs onto canvas)

Canvas–any mesh size between 14 and 18 mesh per inch; a piece large enough for whatever project you want to try

Masking tape–½″ to ¾″ wide to bind edges of canvas

Yarns, needles, thimble, scissors

I.D. TAGS

These can be used for luggage tags or key rings. Use penelope canvas, as it is sturdier for finishing the edges; mono canvas for this particular project does not work as well. Along with the basic materials, you'll need a strap for a luggage tag or a ring for keys. Watch straps work well for the luggage tags.

There are several layouts for tags that you can use, but you can make up your own—the techniques do not change. The important thing to remember when laying out your design is that the front and back must have exactly the same dimensions so that they will match when they are joined.

1. Lay tracing paper over letter or letters you want on one side of the tag, and trace. Design one side of

your tag and then the other, using the same dimensions and leaving ⅛″ in the center between the two sides. Outline your final design in black.

2. Cut out your canvas about 1″ larger all around than your design. Bind the edges with masking tape. Trace your design onto the canvas, using the canvas threads as guidelines to keep the design straight. In the center, between the two sides, mark the area to be left open for the strap or ring to go through. Carefully cut between your marks on each side of the tag. Stitch in your design, stitching over the cut edges where the strap is to go. Block the tag flat.

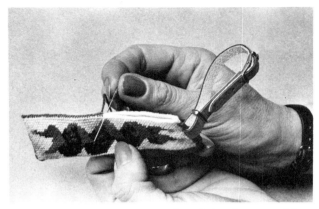

Buttonhole-stitch all around to join the two sides; the stitch has already been made over the cut section where the strap goes through.

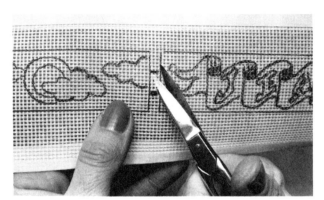

Cut between the two sides where the strap or ring will go through; ALPHABET 5 on the right.

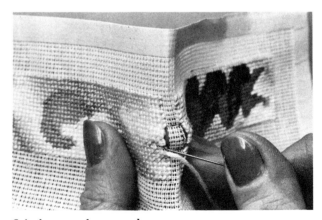

Stitch over the cut edges.

Key ring with a single initial from ALPHABET 4

3. Trim excess canvas, leaving about ¼″ all around. Turn edges in and press flat. Fold tag in half at the center; and go around the four sides with the buttonhole stitch, joining the two sides together. Start stitching them together at the end opposite the fold. Continue all around, keeping the stitches close together and, when you get to the fold, continue making the buttonhole stitch over the section of canvas where you cut to make the opening for the strap.

4. Put the strap through the finished opening so it can be attached to a bag or whatever you want it to go on.

STRIPS

Strips include belts, chokers, bracelets, napkin rings, bookmarks, backing for clear plastic paper-weights, and so on, or anything that is fairly narrow and has clean-finished edges.

Once you decide what you want, make your paper pattern and design pattern. For a belt, you can tape paper together to make the pattern long enough. For all of the items, stitch in your needle-point design, block, trim excess canvas, and finish the edges with the buttonhole stitch. It's easier to block before you trim away the canvas, because you can grasp the taped edges to pull it into shape.

Gluing felt on the back of a bookmark

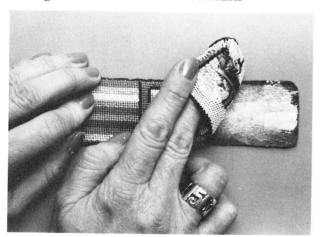

To finish the back of the pieces (if the back is going to show), use felt or ribbon. Felt works well because you can cut it to any shape you want and leave the edges unfinished because it won't fray. Always cut the felt slightly smaller than the finished area. Glue it in place, spreading the glue on the wrong side of the felt. You can also slip-stitch it in place along the edge. Ribbon can also be used if it's the right width.

Finished bookmark; monogram, ALPHABET 2

Belts.

Along with basic materials, you'll need a buckle, backing, and eyelets. To estimate a length for a belt, take the waist measurement and add about 6″. Use a width that will fit the size of the buckle you choose. If you are using a harness

Putting a harness buckle and belt loop on a finished needlepoint belt; line the belt after the buckle is secured.

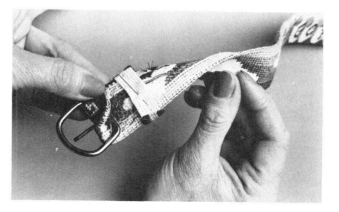

buckle, you will need a belt loop to hold the flap of the belt in place when it is buckled. Make one in needlepoint by stitching a very narrow strip, or use leather or ribbon. Once the edges have been finished, put the buckle on one end, fold back the end over the buckle (if there's a prong, stick it through the needlepoint), and stitch the flap in place. Cover the back with whatever you want and, if you want eyelets, put them in last.

Napkin Rings.

Buy a wooden or plastic ring to cover. Get one wide enough to make room for a design. Measure the width and circumference, and lay out your pattern. Stitch in the design and, after you block it and trim the canvas, join the ends together to form a ring. Then fold back and finish the edges with the buttonhole stitch. Slip this over the napkin ring. Place a few drops of glue on the back of the needlepoint to hold it in place.

Chokers, Bracelets.

Work these items the way you work belts, but use hooks and eyes for closings. If you are using any decorative beads, put them on before you put the backing on.

Choker ready to be lined. The multicolored pattern is derived from the beads sewn to the edge of the choker. (The beads are imported from India and are available in most craft shops that carry a good stock of beads.)

Napkin ring; monogram, ALPHABET 5

Paperweight Backings, Bookmarks.

You can buy weighted, clear-plastic frames in the picture-frame section of any department store. Instead of putting in a photo, trace off the outline of the area for the photo, and make a needlepoint design to fit the space. Finish the edges all around with the buttonhole stitch, and slip under the plastic.

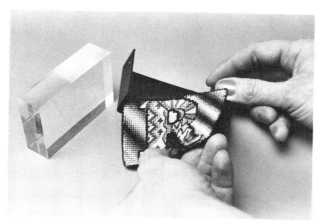

Clear-plastic picture frame serves as a paperweight with a needlepoint backing; initial, ALPHABET 3. The background is stitched with a shaded cotton floss that goes from light to dark and back to light all in the same thread.

I. D. tags

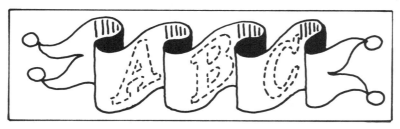

Alphabet 5

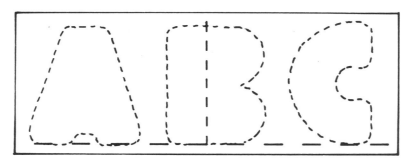

Alphabet 2

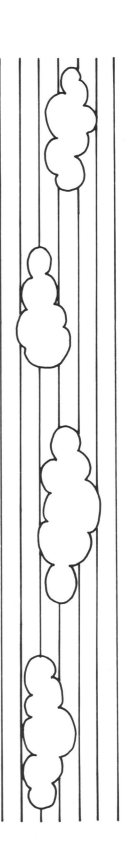

Bookmarks

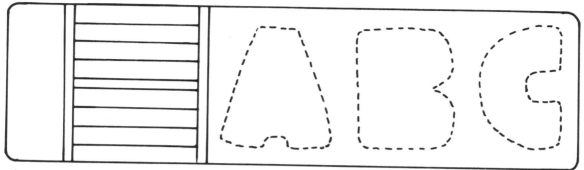

ALPHABET 2

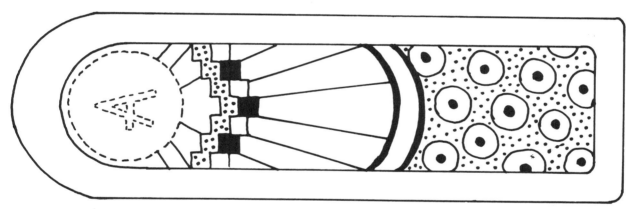

ALPHABET 10

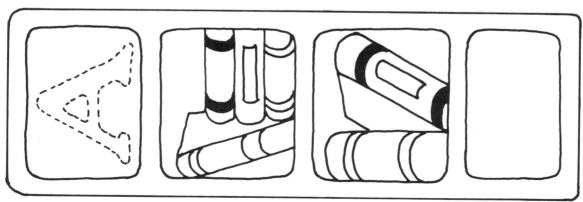

ALPHABET 4

Strip patterns for frames, belts, chokers   Pattern for choker on page 34

COVERS, HOLDERS

The same methods are used for a bookend cover as are used to make a coin purse—in both cases you are creating a pouch, one to go over something and the other to be filled with something. The following are a few suggestions for things you can make.

Bookend Covers.

Metal bookends are available in office-supply and stationery stores. They are gray metal, not very fancy, but they work very well. There are also letter holders and file holders that are similar in design. They can all be covered. If you want to paint the metal, do so before you put on the needlepoint.

1. Make a paper pattern of the area to be covered. Make your design pattern, and transfer the design to canvas; allow about 2 extra rows of needlepoint around the top and sides for turning.

Bookend needlepoint is buttonhole-stitched at the bottom and then machine-sewn to the fabric backing.

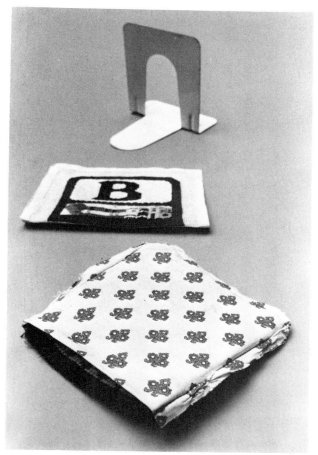

2. Block and trim excess canvas, leaving about ½". Turn back the bottom edge and finish across with buttonhole stitch.

3. Cut a piece of fabric the same size as your needlepoint, and hem the bottom edge of the fabric. With right sides facing each other and the bottom edges lined up, stitch around three sides with a sewing machine, using the needlepoint side

Metal bookends may be painted to match your design.

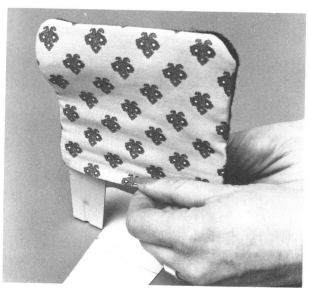

This bookend design is taken from ALPHABET 4.

as the guide for the stitching line. Turn right side out, press, and slip over the bookend or letter holder.

Letter holder. Similar to a bookend in design, the needlepoint here is sewn to a piece of fabric cut to cover and to be glued to the entire surface of the holder, inside and out. Initial is from ALPHABET 1.

Designs for small squares have many uses—not only holders such as sachets, but also pocket patches with finished edges or inserts for ready-made items such as this mini-album.

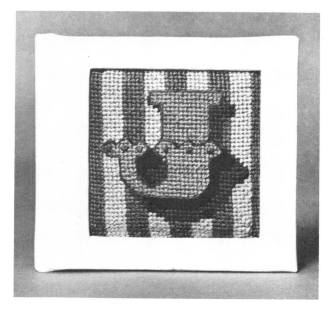

Sachets.

To make a sachet, follow the directions for a bookend, but have the opening at the top instead of at the bottom. Fill it with potpourri, and close the open end by stitching. If you want the sachet to hang, attach a ribbon loop at the top and ribbon streamers at the bottom.

Coin Purses, Makeup Holders.

A rectangle about 4½″ × 7″ seems to be a good size to serve as a small purse or makeup holder, but you can make it any size you wish. You'll need a zipper the length of the opening on one of the long sides. You'll also need fabric for the back and the lining.

1. Make your design pattern, stitch in the design, and block and trim canvas.

2. Cut a piece of fabric the same size for the back and, if you want a lining, cut a piece equal to the front and back together.

Sew the zipper between the needlepoint and the fabric backing, then open the zipper a little before closing the other three sides.

40

3. Baste the zipper between the needlepoint and the fabric, and stitch on at each side with a sewing machine. Press lightly so the edges are flat. Unzip the zipper slightly. Now stitch around the other three edges, joining the needlepoint front and fabric back. Trim seam, clip the corners, and turn.

4. For the lining, fold the second piece of fabric in half, right side in, and stitch the side seams closed. Turn, fold back a hem along the top, and place the lining inside the purse. Fasten the lining to the purse along the zipper with a slip stitch.

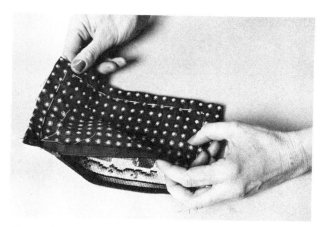

Open the zipper all the way and turn the purse right side out; the lining will cover the wrong side of the needlepoint.

Fasten the lining with a slip stitch.

Finished purse; monogram, ALPHABET 1.

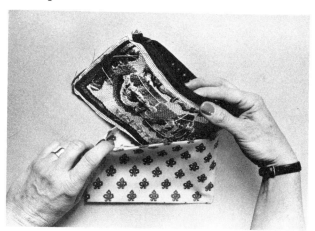

ALPHABET 4

ALPHABET 1

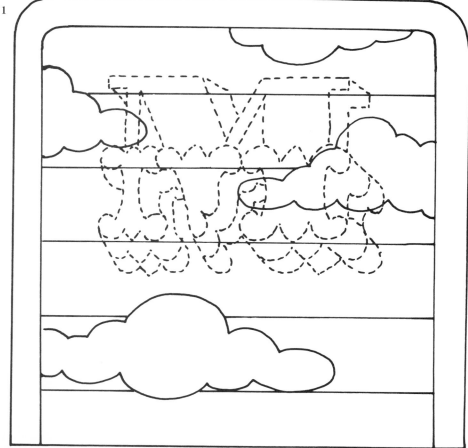

Bookend covers

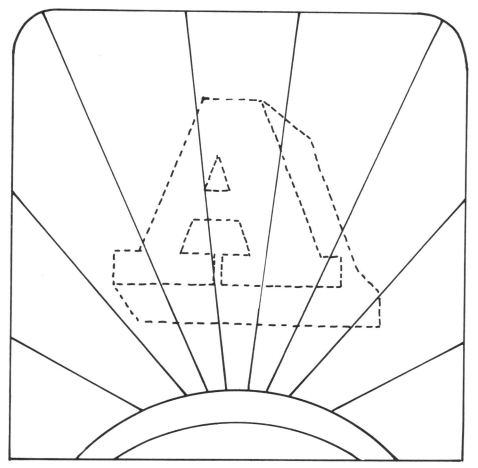

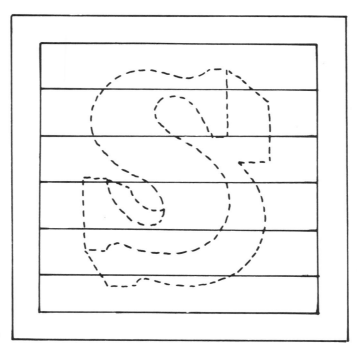

Squares for sachets, plastic-frame paperweights, clean-finished patches, or mini-album inserts

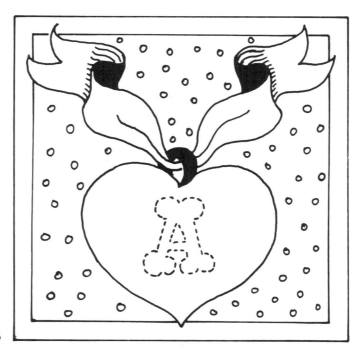

Coin Purse

Coin Purse

ALPHABETS 6 and 7

46

CHRISTMAS ORNAMENTS & PINCUSHIONS

All of these designs are circles; the larger ones can be used interchangeably for ornaments or pincushions. Along with the basic materials, you'll need a piece of cardboard to back the ornaments, felt, and pieces of ribbon to hang them. You'll need a pincushion to cover if you wish to make that.

1. Make design pattern, trace, stitch, and block. Trim excess canvas, leaving ½″ to ¾″ around the edge.

2. Cut out a piece of stiff cardboard about ⅛″ less all around than the finished size of the needlepoint. Use a compass to get an accurate circle.

3. Spread glue on one side of cardboard, and place on the back side of needlepoint, making sure it's centered.

4. Using a threaded length of double floss, go around the edge of extra canvas with a running stitch.

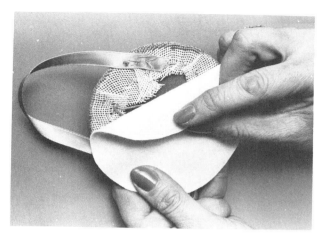

Felt, glued on, covers the gathered canvas and the ends of the ribbon loop.

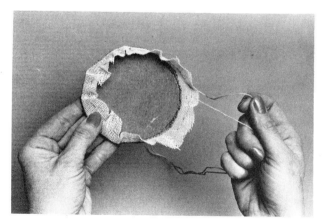

Gathering the excess canvas to the back of the circle

5. Pull threads, gathering all around, and tie with a knot to secure. Press gathers as flat as possible.

6. Cut a piece of ribbon about 10″ long, or as long as you want it, fold in half, and sew to the back side, at the top of the circle. Place the ornament on a piece of felt and trace around the edge. Cut the felt out and spread glue on one side. Place over the

Angel ornament: The stars are stitched in metallic thread and the angel is outlined in the stem stitch.

back of the ornament and press together. If any of the felt shows on the front side, trim the edge once it's glued on.

Wreath ornament: The center of the wreath can be cut out and finished with the buttonhole stitch to frame a picture.

Tree ornament: The tree is decorated with a metallic-thread star and beaded garlands.

Christmas Ornaments

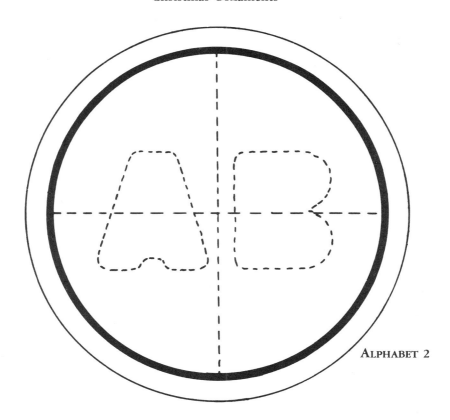

ALPHABET 2

Christmas ornaments

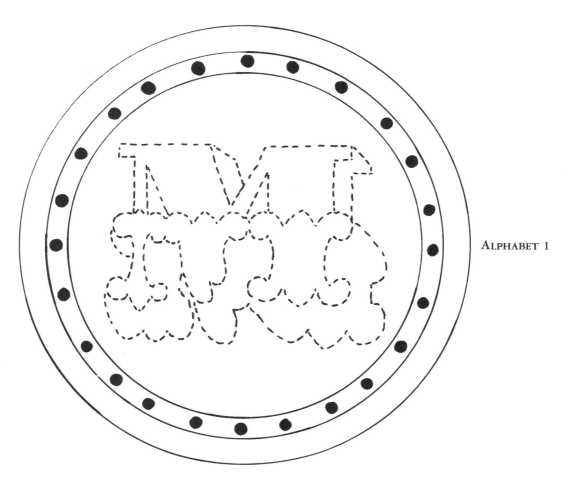

Christmas ornaments

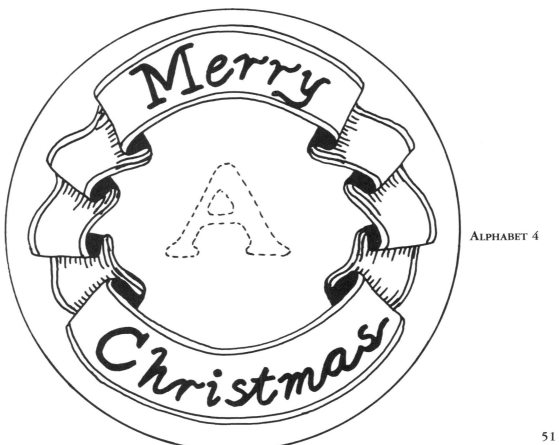

Pincushion

You'll need a small-sized red tomato pincushion found in any dime store. Work it the same way you would work the ornament. Once you have gone around the edge of extra canvas with a running stitch, place the needlepoint over the pincushion (stick a pin in the top center, through the needlepoint, to hold it in place) and pull the thread, gathering the canvas tightly around the pincushion. Tie or stitch the thread to secure it. Cut a small circle of felt to cover the bottom, and glue or stitch in place.

A small circle of felt, sewn or glued on, covers the gathers on the bottom of the finished pincushion.

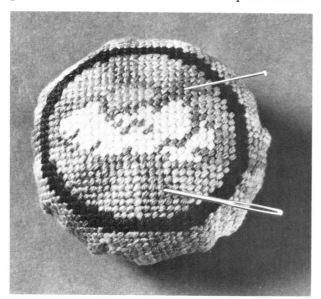

Circle designs can be made to fit boxes such as this one with an inset in the lid made especially for needlepoint. Monogram, ALPHABET 1

Pincushions. These could also be made into sachets
or used for a round box-top insert as on page 52.

MATS, FRAMES

All of the mat-design suggestions will fit into standard-size frames, but the finished size of your mat will depend on what type of frame you'll be putting it in. For a plastic box frame, finish the mat slightly larger than you would for a mat that would go inside a frame. Try your design pattern in the space where you want it to go to be sure it fits. If the mat will be inside a frame, it does not need a clean-finished edge; block it and trim it close so that it lies flat inside the frame. The glass can go behind or in front of the mat. If you use beads, the mat will not stay flat, and so it must go in front of the glass. I prefer mats in front of the glass because they are more visible. For a plastic box frame, clean-finish the edges after you've blocked the needle-point, and then put it inside the frame.

NOTE: Any fabric covering or decoration of the frame should be done before the photos are put in.

1. Make design pattern, transfer it to canvas, stitch, and block. The example here is for a mat for five photos.

2. Trim canvas around photo cutouts, leaving ¼" to ½" for turnback (see page 18). If they are oval or round shapes, clip in all around the turnbacks so they will lie flat. Clean-finish the cutouts with the buttonhole stitch.

Placing the five photos that go behind the mat

3. Place the mat over the piece of cardboard that comes with the frame, and mark the outlines of the openings in pencil. Glue the photos in place on the cardboard. Place the frame face down. Put in either the glass or the mat first, then the photos on the cardboard, then the backing that usually comes with the frame, too.

The needlepoint mat is framed with another mat covered in velvet and a chrome frame.

The cardboard backing of the box frame is covered with checked gingham.

4. For a plastic box frame, cover the cardboard backing as you wish, and secure the photo in place

on the backing. Place the mat over the photo and secure that in place, then slip the plastic cover over it.

The mat opening is ringed with pearl beads. Velvet-covered second mat and chrome frame

Larger needlepoint mat in plastic box frame

Needlepoint mat inside velvet-covered standing frame

Needlepoint-covered standing frame stitched in colors of the needlepoint mat; this is quite difficult to do and after one try, even though successful, I don't really recommend it.

Mat with five openings for family photo
ALPHABET 8

FOR

DADDY

Picture mat
ALPHABET 7

LOVE

JENNIFER

Picture mat
ALPHABET 8

The Voglers

Picture mat
ALPHABET 8

Carolyn & Dan

April 1977

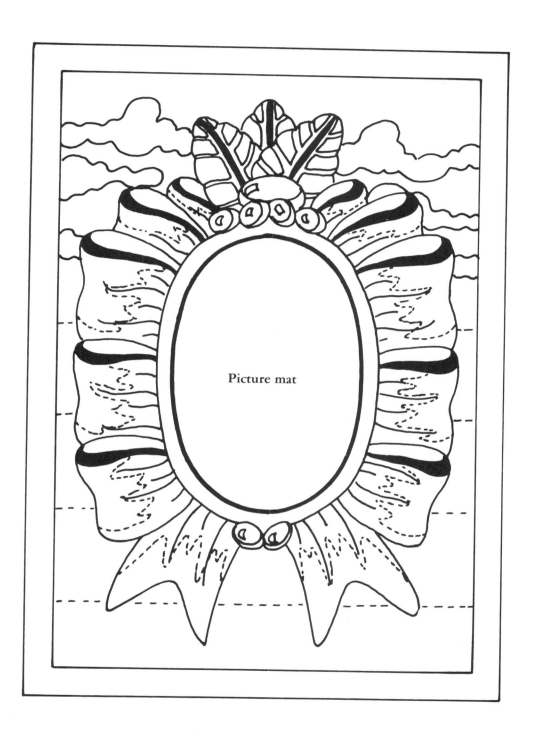

Picture mat

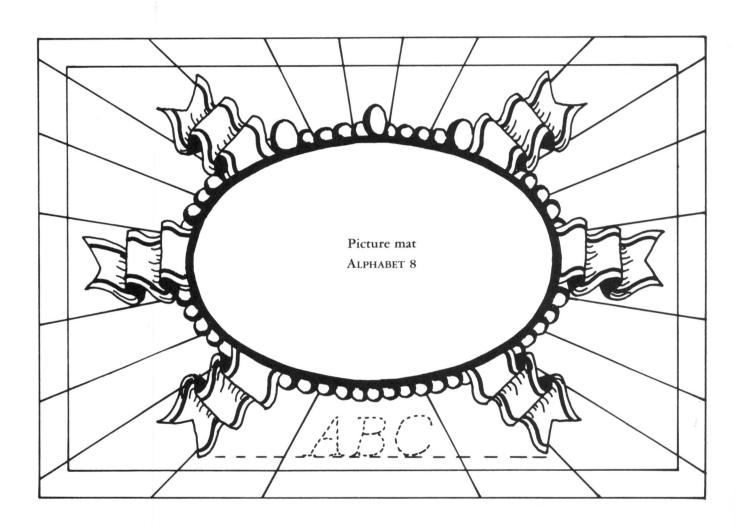

Picture mat
ALPHABET 8

Picture mat
ALPHABET 8

Frame pattern; see page 22

Alphabet 10

Picture mat
ALPHABET 7

Gregory Townsend
Gladstone
Feb 13 1972

BOXES

Any type of box can be covered, but the easiest to work with are square, flat boxes made of wood. Use needlepoint on both top and bottom or on the top only.

1. Make a paper pattern for the box you want to cover and fill in the areas for needlepoint with a design pattern. Your design pattern should end just inside the edges of the box, so that when the piece is finished with the buttonhole edge, it will fit to the edge of the box exactly.

NOTE: If the box is to be lined or painted, do this before you put on the needlepoint.

2. Stitch in your design and block. Cut excess canvas from corners and snip in so the corner seam will fold flat. Clean-finish the edges with the buttonhole stitch.

Needlepoint box top with edges finished and canvas trimmed at the corners

3. Spread glue on the box top, or bottom, and place the needlepoint on it. Put in pushpins right through the needlepoint to hold it in place. Spread glue on sides of box, and press needlepoint against

them, folding in the raw edges at each corner. Hold the sides in place with pushpins. Join the corners together with yarn, and secure it by running it back through the seam. Snip it off closely. Leave the pushpins in place until the glue is dry.

Joining the corner seam of the box top; start at the edge and work up to the corner.

4. To put the hinges on, place the lid on the box, tie a string around it as you would tie a package to hold the two halves together; keep the top and bottom properly lined up. Place the hinges on the back of the box and screw them in place.

Finished box top; initials, ALPHABET 6; lettering, ALPHABET 7

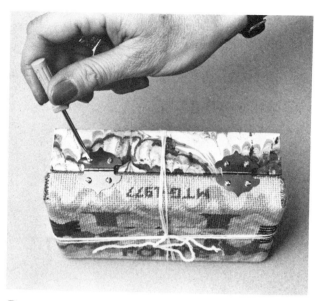

Bottom and inside of box were covered with marbleized paper; needlepoint background was stitched in wavy bands of color picked up from the paper. Last step is to put on the hinges.

Box lid

ALPHABET 7 and ALPHABET 6; see photo, page 66

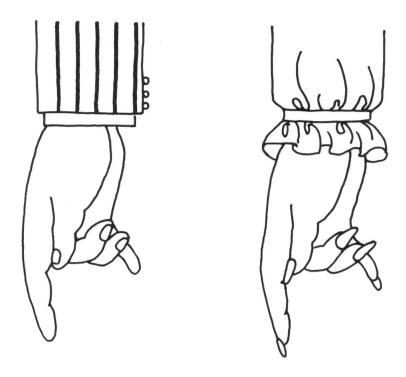

Different hands for use with ALPHABET 6

ALBUM COVERS

Any type of hardcover album can be covered. I suggest, however, that you cover one with a ring binder inside so that it can be used for a long time, and you can change the pages if you wish.

1. Make a paper pattern of the album to be covered, and make your design pattern (see page 26). Allow about ½" extra needlepoint all around your pattern so that when it's turned back, there won't be any raw canvas showing.

2. Stitch in your design and block into shape, making sure it's squared out accurately. Trim excess canvas, leaving about ½" all around. Lay the needlepoint, right side down, on your work surface.

3. Spread glue over the entire outside cover of the album, and let it dry for a moment until it is tacky to the touch. Open the cover flat and lay it, glue side down, on the needlepoint.

4. The edges of the needlepoint must be turned back onto the inside of the cover. Spread glue around inside edges, bend in the needlepoint, and use pushpins to secure in place. Sew the corners together so that they lie flat. Allow glue to dry completely.

5. Use felt or leather to finish the inside panels. Spread glue on the back sides of the two pieces of lining, place them on the inside of the cover, and press smooth with your hands.

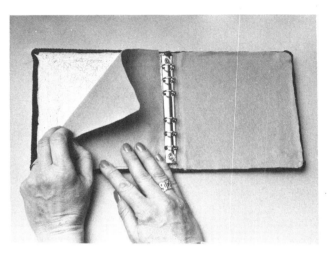

A felt or leather lining is glued to the inside panels of the cover. Monogram, ALPHABET 10

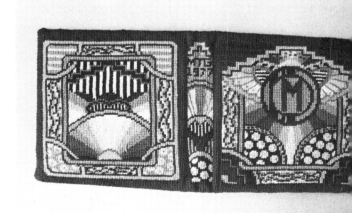

Gluing down the turnback of the needlepoint album cover.

Album cover, front

For initial in circle, ALPHABET 10

Album cover, back

MINI-PILLOWS

The following designs are all for small pillows, and there is a choice of four different shapes to make. They can all be personalized with initials or monograms, dates, messages, and could be framed as well as made into pillows. Once you decide what shape you want, make your design pattern. Put in the letters, names, dates, or whatever special personal object you wish to add. Use the alphabets suggested, or feel free to do your own thing. Transfer your design to the canvas.

Stitch in the needlepoint, block into shape, and trim away the excess canvas.

Mini-pillow
ALPHABET 3

73

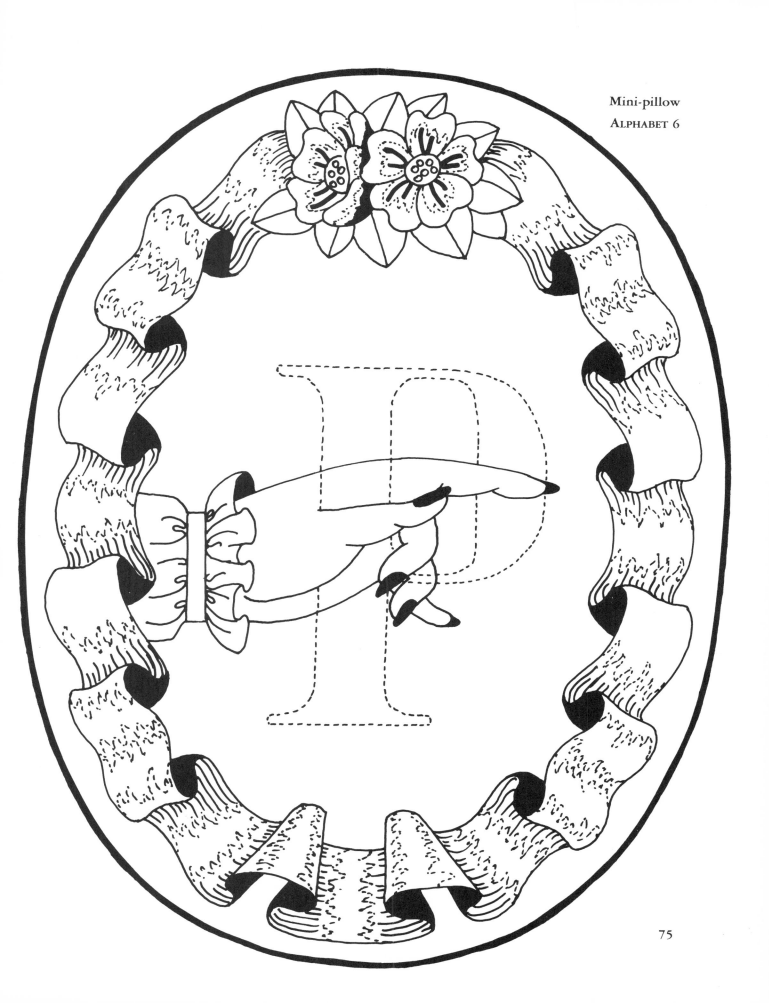

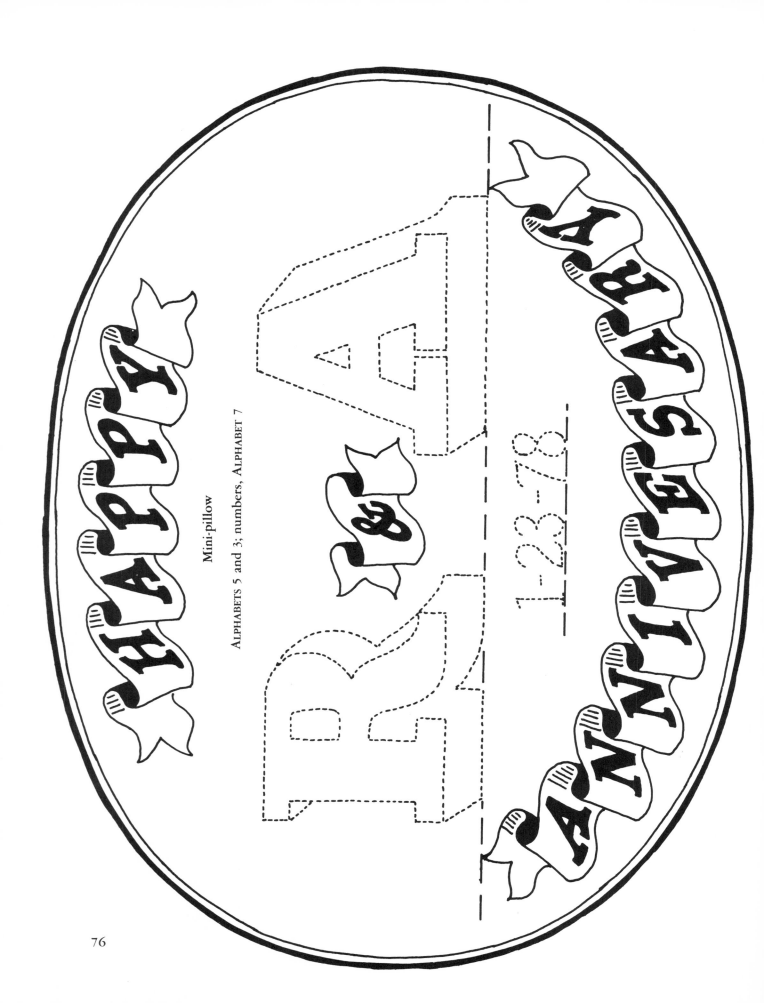

Mini-pillow

ALPHABETS 5 and 3; numbers, ALPHABET 7

Mini-pillow
ALPHABET 9

HAPPY BIRTHDAY

Mini-pillow design based on ALPHABET 4

ABCDEFGHIJKL
MNOPQRSTUVW
XYZ

PILLOW FORMS AND COVERS

You can have your pillow made professionally, but try making it yourself. Because the shapes and sizes are not standard, you'll need to make a pillow form to fit the shape. Both the needlepoint cover and the form are made the same way. You'll need muslin and stuffing for the form and fabric for the backing of the pillow.

All the pillows can be made flat (knife-edged) or boxed, but for these small sizes I prefer the boxed shape. Boxed pillows are more complicated to make than flat ones, but with a little time and patience, they are worth making yourself.

1. For a pillow form, cut one front and one back in the shape of the needlepoint pillow design, allowing ½" seams all around. Cut a strip of muslin 2½" wide and long enough to go around the outside edge of the entire pillow.* The strip will be the piece that goes between the front and back and will make the box shape. For the pillow cover, cut one back and one strip in the fabric you've decided on for the backing of the needlepoint. I'll use the circle shape for the example.

* NOTE: Cut strip 25" long for the circle; 23" long for the semicircle; 28½" long for the oval; 29" long for the square.

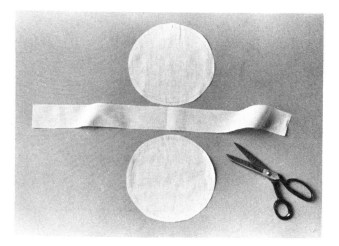

Muslin front, back, and side strip for the pillow form; also cut one back and one strip in the fabric you choose for the needlepoint backing.

2. Join the strip that goes between the front and back with a seam so that it becomes a continuous strip. Join the strip to the pillow front all around with a ½" seam. Now join the strip to the back,

Boxing strip and front, joined

leaving a section open so that it can be turned and stuffed. Turn, stuff, pin the opening shut, and slip-stitch by hand.

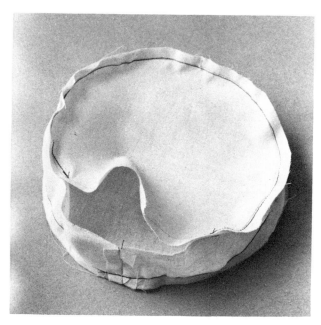

Pillow form with back partly joined

The needlepoint pillow cover is made the same way, but leave a space open at the back large enough so that the cover can be slipped over the form. Then slip-stitch closed.

NOTE: For a flat or knife-edge pillow, simply sew the front and back together, leaving an opening so that it can be turned and stuffed.

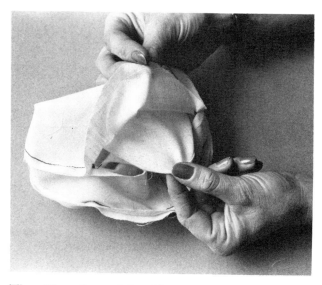

The pillow form right side out, stuff, pin together, and slip-stitch to close.

Needlepoint pillow cover is made just like the pillow form; leave opening large enough in the backing to be able to put in the form, and slip-stitch to close. Initial, ALPHABET 3

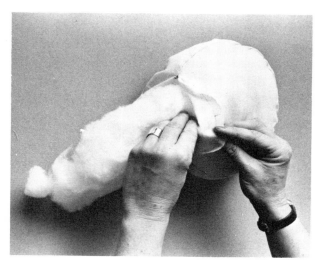

hen using the fine-mesh canvases recommended in this book, the letters of these alphabets may be traced directly onto the canvas and stitched following the outlines rather than counted out stitch for stitch.

ALPHABET 1

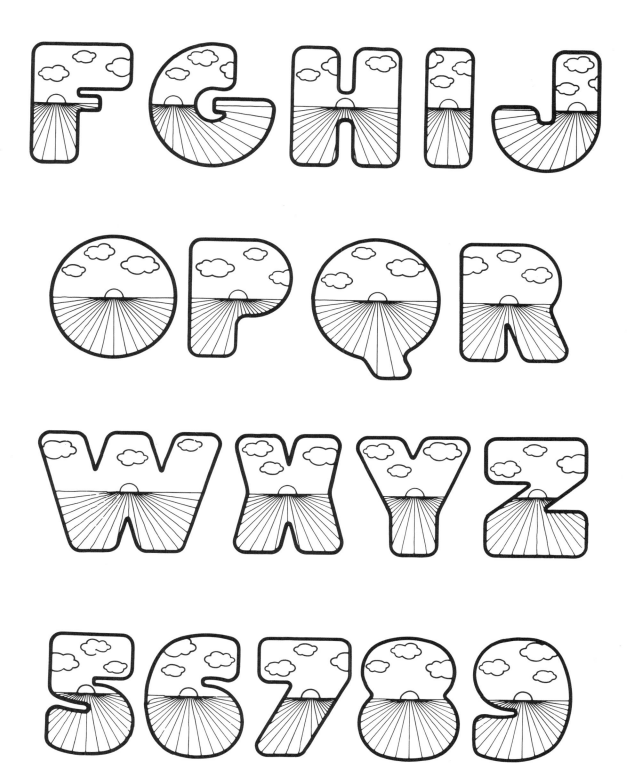

A B

E F

I J

C D

G H

K L

M N
Q R
U V

P O
S T
W

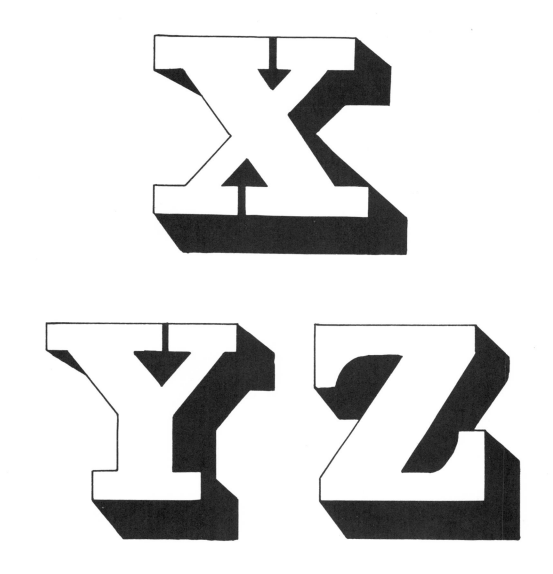

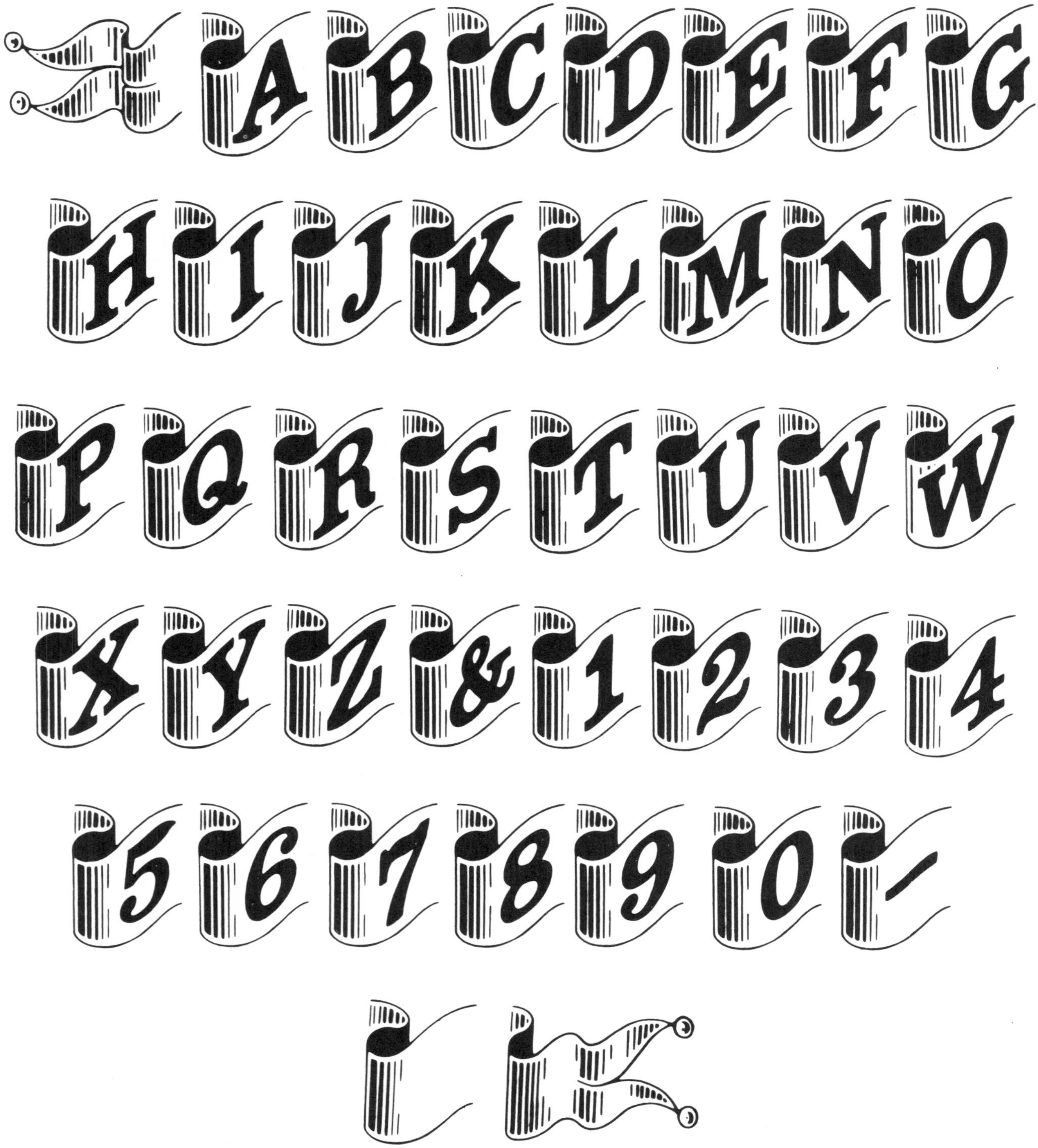

A B C D E F G
H I J K L M N O
P Q R S T U V W
X Y Z & 1 2 3 4
5 6 7 8 9 0 —

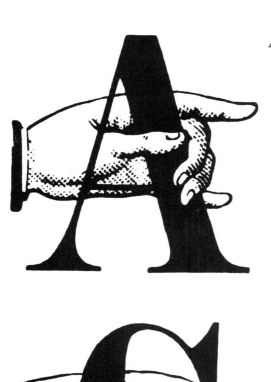

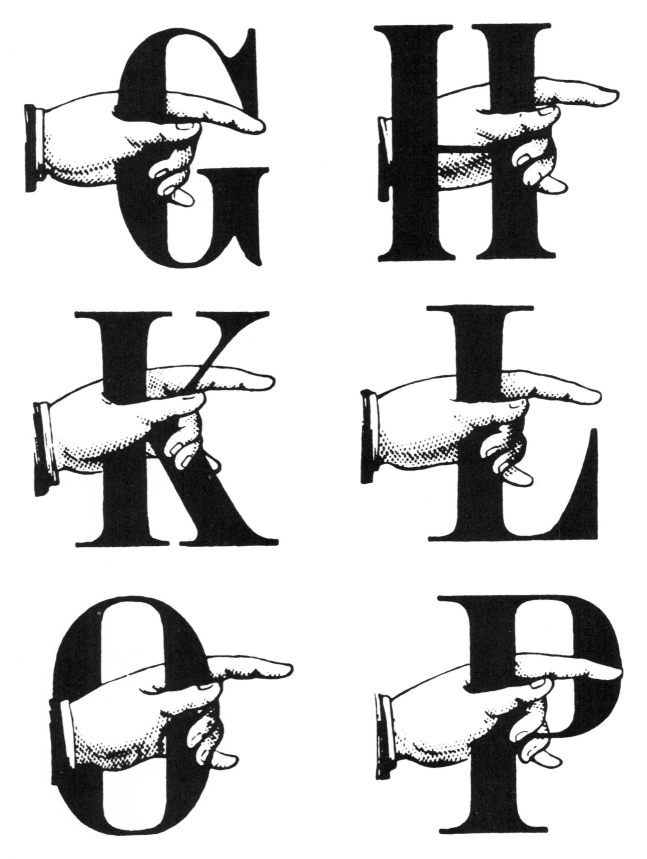

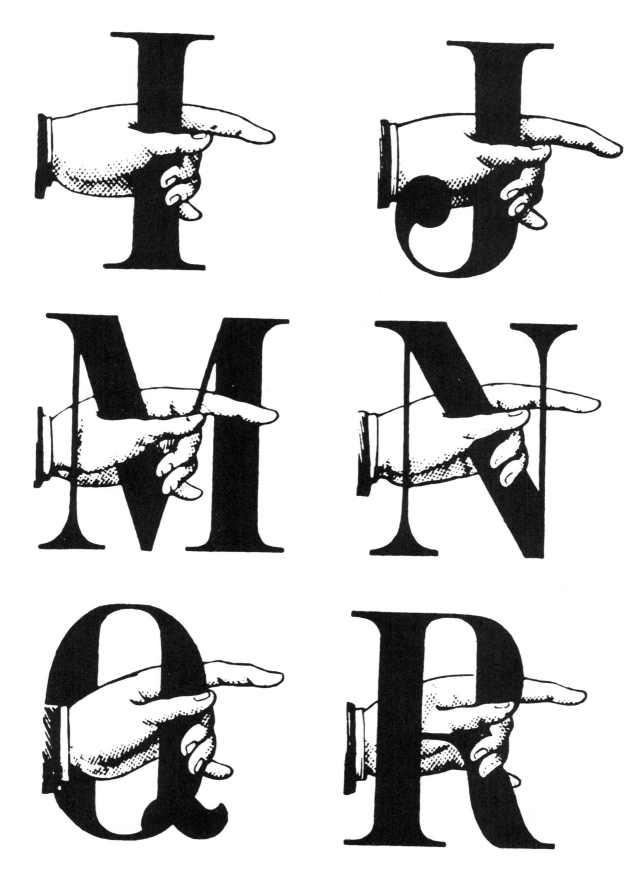

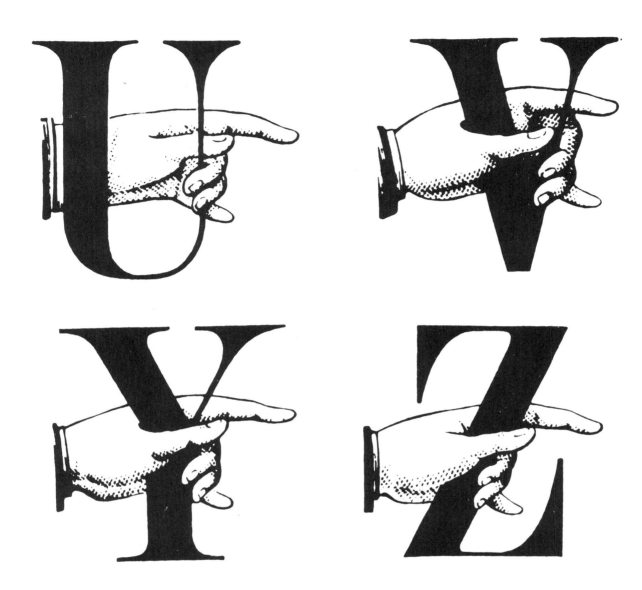

ABCDEFGHIJKLMN
OPQRSTUVWXYZ&
abcdefghijklmnopqrstuv
wxyz 1234567890

ABCDEFGHIJKLMNOP
QRSTUVWXYZ&
abcdefghijklmnopqrstuvwxyz
123456789

A B C D E F G
H I J K L M N
O P Q R S T U V
W X Y Z

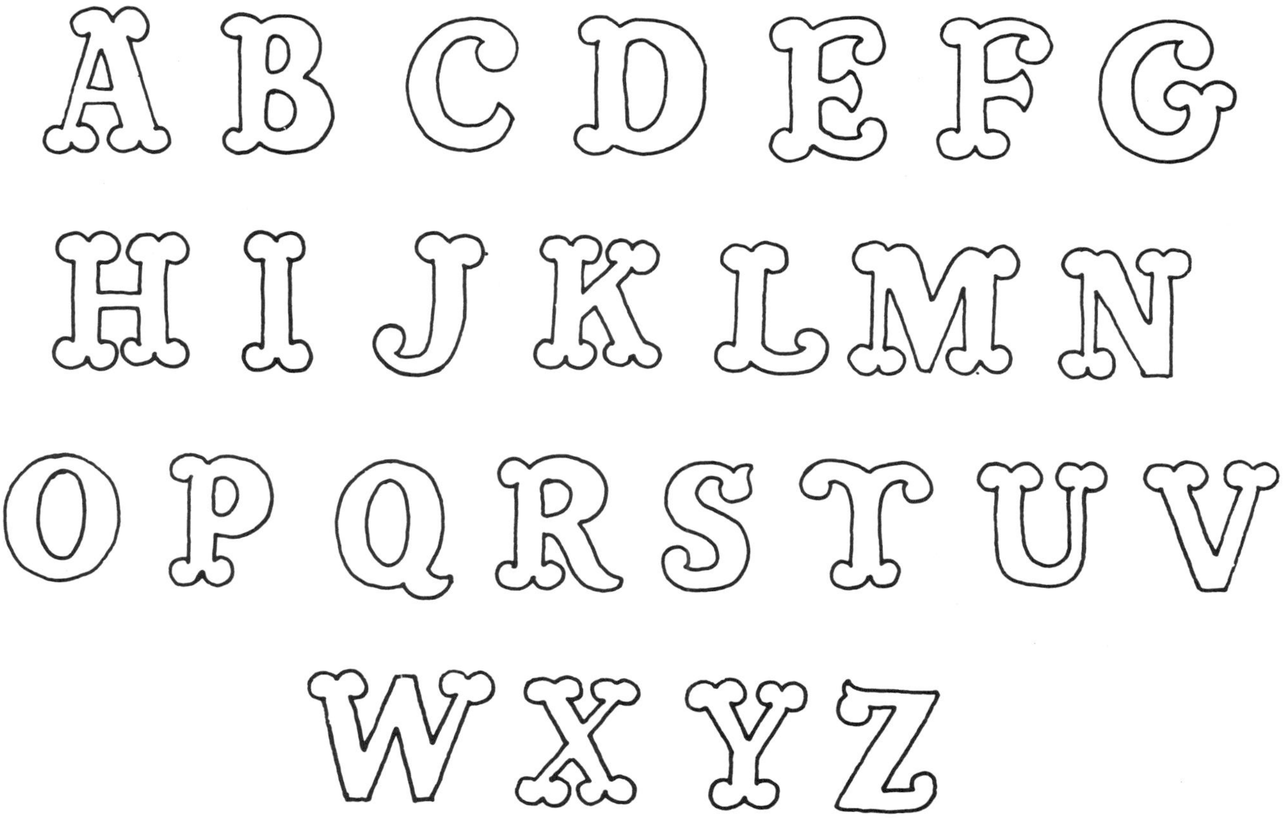

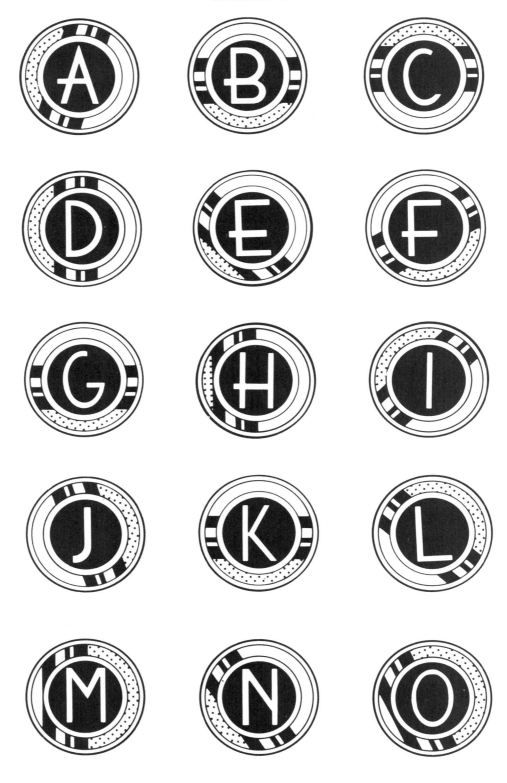

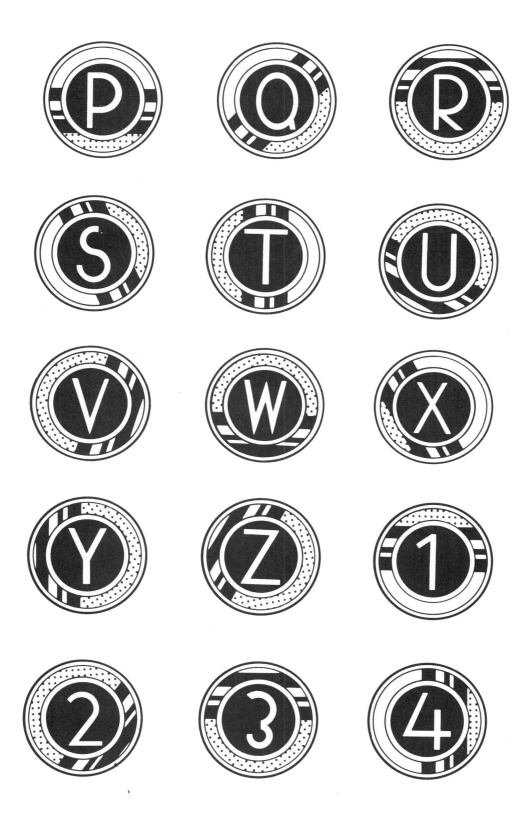

ABCDEFGHIJKLM
NOPQRSTUVWXY
Z - 1234567890.

The Monstre Alphabet

The "Monstre" alphabet that starts on page 115 is a bonus printed here because I have had so many requests from readers who have my *Needlepoint Alphabet Book* asking for a full-scale version that does not have to be blown up by photostat to be transferred to canvas. This one, reprinted from my sewing book, *Kids' Clothes by Meredith Gladstone,* can be traced directly onto fine-mesh canvases such as 14- or 16-mesh. Any single letter would make a perfect, extra-small mini-pillow, or a box top, or two letters could be used for the front and back of a small album cover. In the white spaces at the bottom of the letters, you could embroider a name or your signature initials. And surely you can think of still more ideas of your own for using the letters. The one thing to remember in tracing them is that the vertical and horizontal lines must be traced to align with the vertical and horizontal threads of the canvas.

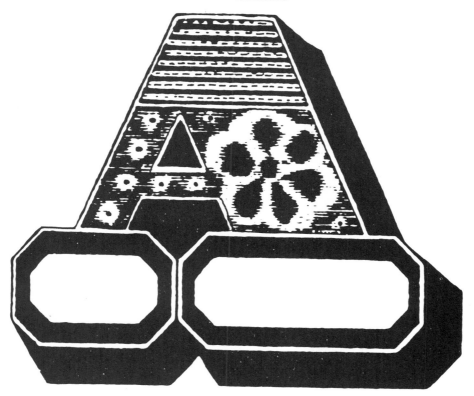

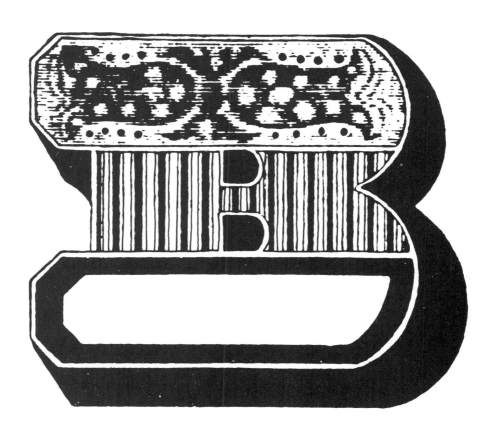

115

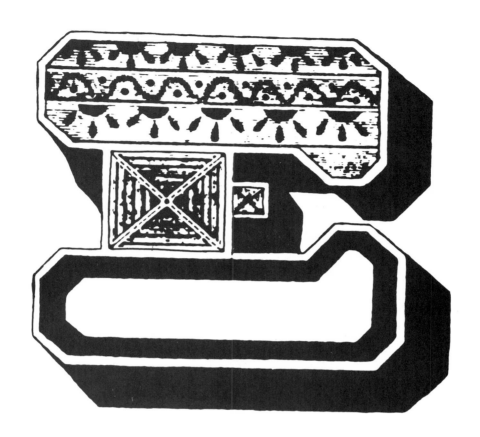

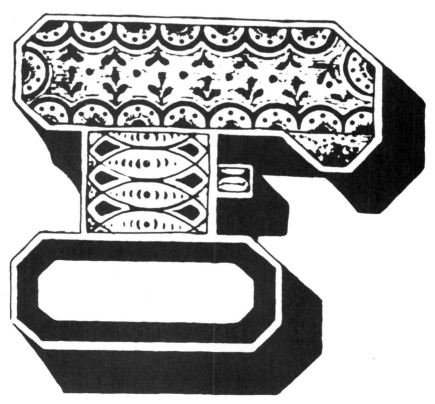

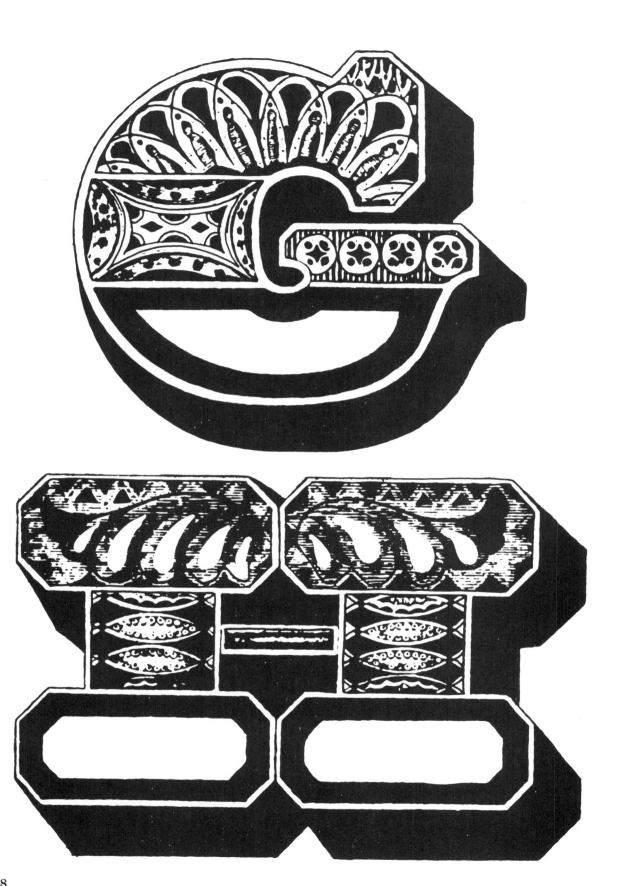

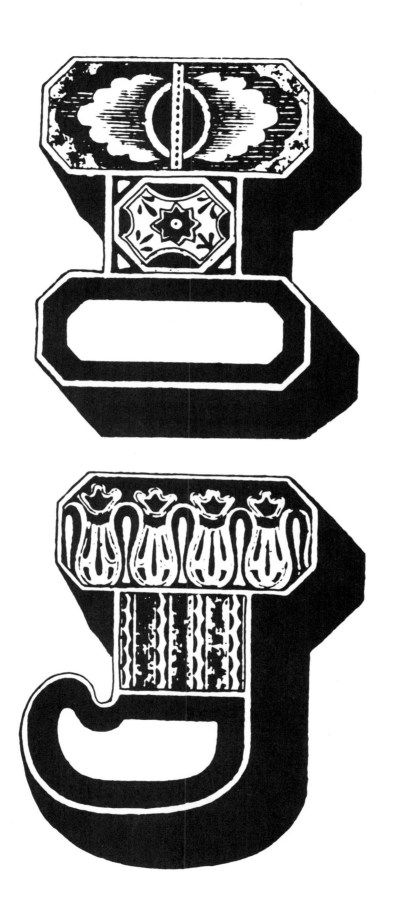

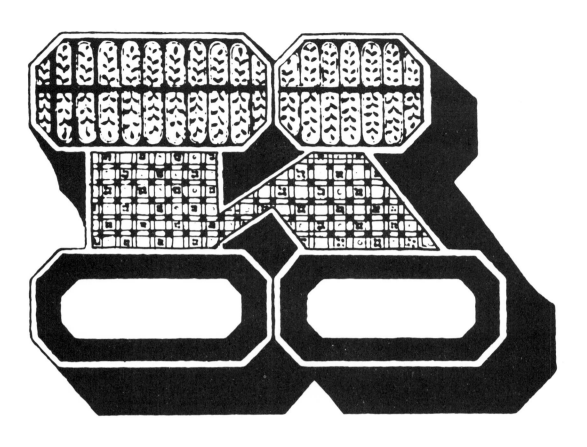

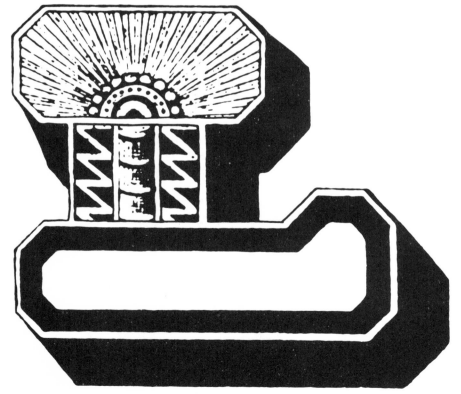

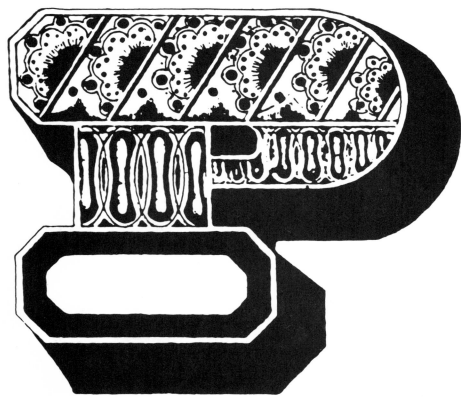

123

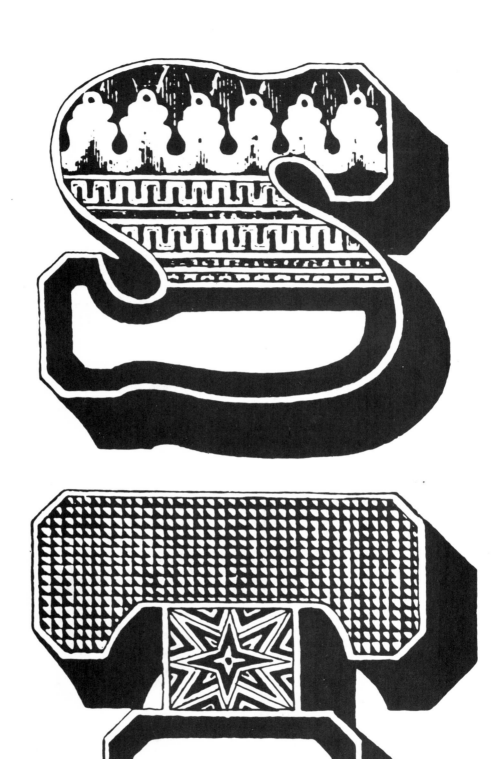

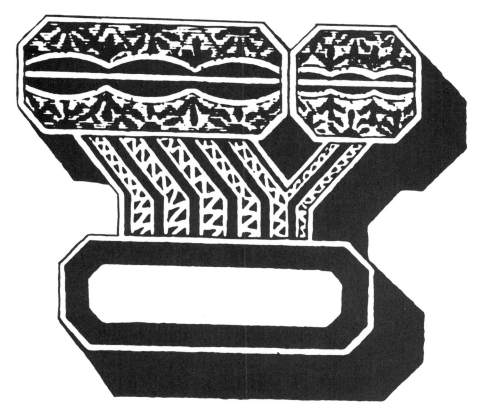

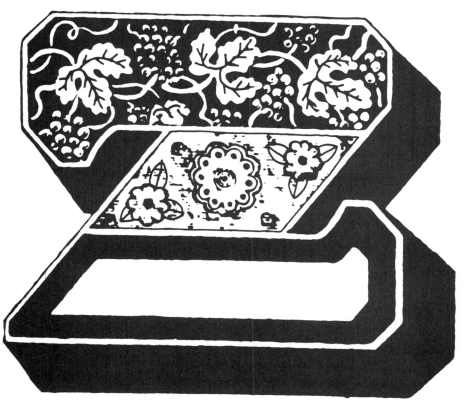

Index